Glynn Christian

Radio and Cookbook

Futura
Macdonald & Co
London & Sydney

A Futura Book

First published as *The LBC Radio Cookbook* 1981 by
Jill Norman & Hobhouse Ltd

First Futura edition 1983

Copyright © Glynn Christian 1981

All rights reserved
No part of this publication may be reproduced,
stored in a retrieval system, or transmitted, in any
form or by any means without the prior
permission in writing of the publisher, nor be
otherwise circulated in any form of binding or
cover other than that in which it is published and
without a similar condition including this
condition being imposed on the subsequent
purchaser.

ISBN 0 7088 2438 2

Reproduced, printed and bound in Great Britain by
Hazell Watson & Viney Limited,
Member of the BPCC Group,
Aylesbury, Bucks

Futura Publications
A Division of
Macdonald & Co (Publishers) Ltd
Maxwell House
74 Worship Street
London EC2A 2EN

A BPCC plc Company

Contents

INTRODUCTION	5
STARTERS AND SOUPS	7
MAIN COURSES	27
PUDDINGS AND CAKES	55
Index	77

Introduction

Dear Listener,

Is there a Glynn Christian style? There must be. But this is the first time I've had to identify it.

I suppose the biggest difference between me and most other food people is that over three-quarters of my recipes are original. To some degree they have to be because of the restrictions of radio: not too many ingredients; no complicated techniques. Yet this simple approach is how I've always cooked.

I've never taken a cooking lesson and thus am not unduly influenced by the past. I have enormous respect for the chefs and dishes of the classic cuisine – celebrations of a life I missed – but little is added to the flavour of a coq au vin by having a boy spend hours peeling baby onions; chicken breasts can be delicious without truffle stuffing and cocks'-comb garnishes. We no longer have the money, the staff or the taste for them.

This is not to say I am against convenience foods, or that I never look backwards. Without knowledge of the good things of the past we have little hope of excellence in the future. I loathe the 'open a tin of tomato soup' school of food. I regret that English tourists in Spain complain the local chicken is too 'strong'; it's actually real, free-range chicken, but their palates have been sadly reduced to accepting only battery-reared blandness. And I curse the army of starched Home Economists who have removed the fun from food, packaging a parade of pre-processed foods with cute names and parsley sprigs, but which owe little to nature and know nothing of honesty. Cooking is an art. Those who wish to make it a science should be sent packing.

I use a lot of exotic ingredients – green peppercorns, rosewater, ginger root and so on. But what's the point of seeing them without knowing what to do with them?

INTRODUCTION

Judicious use of something different can transform the taste of simple food for extraordinarily little effort or cost.

Sometimes I use expensive ingredients. Pheasant, a whole salmon, or leg of lamb. Why not? Hundreds of food writers hark on about economy and economical dishes. I'm sick of being told I'm poor. I know that. Surely someone has to talk about the good times? Judging by many of the recipes in this collection – selected for the book because they were the ones most requested by listeners – I know a lot of you agree.

I think my style is based on achieving an uncomplicated but fascinating flavour with minimal ingredients, attention to balance and presentation, and a refusal to compete with restaurant food or other writers. I don't believe in complicated vegetables. I like to serve very simple vegetables with a special meat, poultry or fish dish. I always put a sauce under or around food (unless I'm ashamed of its appearance). It looks better and it allows each component of the dish to be tasted separately. And I always serve cheese before pudding.

There are hundreds of recipes and tips I'd like to give you, but some just aren't suitable for broadcasting. Clamour for them! Then perhaps there'll be a bigger, more comprehensive book than this.

As in everything else, there are clichés in food. Bacon and eggs are a cliché. So are strawberries and cream. Yet who would refuse them? They are *right*. My overall view of food is also a cliché – food should be fun: fun to make, fun to eat, and fun to talk about. I know that is right too.

Thanks for listening.

GLYNN CHRISTIAN

Starters and Soups

STARTERS AND SOUPS

Parsnip and Cinnamon Soup

Serves 4–6 people

1 lb (450 g) parsnips, at least
2 oz (60 g) butter
salt and cayenne pepper to taste
2 pints (1.2 litres) Jersey milk *or* a mixture of milk and chicken stock
2 fresh bayleaves *or* 1 dry
ground cinnamon
whipped *or* liquid cream

Peel and roughly chop the parsnips, and discard any woody cores, replacing these with better pieces to make up the full 1 lb (450 g) weight. Cook the parsnip pieces gently in the butter in a covered pan with the seasoning until starting to soften (no more than 5 minutes). Add half the liquid with the bayleaves, and cook covered for another 15 minutes.

Liquidise the parsnip mixture, strain through a fine sieve and stir into the remaining milk or stock. Flavour lightly with cinnamon. The exact amount will depend upon the freshness of your spice, but start with ½ teaspoon and go on from there. Correct the overall flavouring with further salt and cayenne if necessary.

To enjoy this pale and interesting soup hot, reheat it and add a generous dollop of chilled whipped cream to each bowl plus a sprinkle of ground cinnamon.

To serve chilled, cool, then refrigerate for at least 4 hours. If it is too thick, stir in some milk. Once the soup is in the bowl, pour in some liquid cream and swirl it with the tip of a teaspoon to create a marbled effect. Sprinkle with cinnamon.

If you are not serving oranges elsewhere in the meal, a pinch of grated orange peel is an interesting addition; so is a thin slice of lemon.

*Parsnips are sweeter and more golden after the first frosts, but they can be the basis of this elegant soup long before then. I first served this soup chilled in autumn when I ran a bistro in Northwood, Middlesex. Once winter arrived, it was equally popular hot.

If you let the soup simmer uncovered so that it reduces, it becomes a sensational sauce for thick slices of grilled ham or for hot salt beef. In fact, if you have a small portion of soup left over, it's good as a sauce for all manner of things, fish and other vegetables included.

STARTERS AND SOUPS

Jerusalem Artichoke Soup with Italian Dressing

Serves 6 people – just

3 lb (1.4 kg) Jerusalem
   artichokes
2 tablespoons lemon juice
2 chicken stock cubes
2 pints (1.2 litres) milk

Italian Dressing
6 rashers smoked streaky
   bacon
3 large tomatoes, peeled and
   deseeded *or* 1 14–16 oz
   (400–450 g) tin plum
   tomatoes, drained
4–6 cloves garlic, chopped
6 dessertspoons chopped
   parsley
freshly-ground black pepper
6 teaspoons whipped cream

There are three ways of dealing with the troublesome peeling of these rugged tubers. I can only recommend peeling them before cooking or peeling them after cooking (the third method, sieving after cooking and mashing to get rid of the skins, produces a less bright-looking soup).

First scrub the artichokes to dislodge dirt and grit, then cut larger ones into small pieces. Cook until tender in a covered pan with just enough water to cover plus the lemon juice. Reserve the cooking liquid. (If you have not yet peeled them, allow them to cool first before peeling.)

STARTERS AND SOUPS

Liquidise the artichokes, incorporating all the cooking water, then pass through a fine sieve. Add the chicken stock cubes and milk and simmer uncovered for 30 minutes. Do not boil. Add more milk to lighten the texture if necessary, but do not cover.

While the soup is simmering its way to perfection, make the dressing. Cut the bacon into small squares and cook in an uncovered small pan until the fat is running freely. Add the tomatoes. (It is difficult to de-seed tinned tomatoes and still preserve their chunkiness, but it is worth trying.) Add the chopped garlic and cook until you have a thick mush without any tomato liquid around the edges. Beware of burning or caramelising the tomato mush. I know whereof I speak.

When ready to serve the soup, stir the parsley into the tomato mush and flavour very highly with coarsely-ground black pepper. Keep the sauce warm, but only just, or you will lose the bright colour of the parsley.

Serve each bowl of soup with a generous spoonful of Italian Dressing in the centre, topped with a teaspoonful of whipped cream.

*This dish was taught me by an Italian and I have cooked it all round the world. The pearl-grey soup is a perfect foil for the electric colours of the dressing.

This soup incorporates chicken stock cubes, which is not an ingredient I would normally use, but in this recipe they are essential and excellent.

Tinned tomatoes are not as good as rich, red, real tomatoes (avoid orange 'salad' tomatoes), but as decent tomatoes have such a short season, it is sensible to use tinned as a substitute. (Indeed, in most recipes, tinned tomatoes are infinitely preferable to the rubbish normally sold in our shops all year round.)

STARTERS AND SOUPS

Cream of Fennel Soup

Serves 4–6 people

1 lb (450 g) fennel root,
  trimmed weight (reserve
  the frondy green tops)
juice of 1 lemon
2 oz (60 g) butter
1 medium clove garlic
½ pint (300 ml) strong chicken
  stock *or* 1 chicken stock
  cube and ½ pint (300 ml)
  water
½ pint (300 ml) milk
salt, pepper, nutmeg
thinly sliced lemon

Roughly slice the trimmed fennel, toss in the lemon juice, then cook in the butter in a covered saucepan for 20 minutes, or until well softened. Add the whole, peeled clove of garlic and the stock. Cook for an extra 5 minutes. Liquidise and strain through a fine sieve. Add the milk and simmer gently for 5 minutes.

This is the most ethereal pale green imaginable, so serve in bowls of a contrasting colour. Float a slice of lemon in each bowl and scatter finely-chopped fennel fronds over that.

If you'd like to try this chilled, and I think you should, allow at least 4 hours in the refrigerator, then stir in a little milk if it seems too thick. Serve and garnish as above.

*Once rare and expensive, fennel is now included in the English crop. Most people recognise its crisp liquorice-flavoured flesh in salads and some will have enjoyed it braised; few will recognise it in this guise. Reduced slightly, it makes an original and satisfying sauce for poached fish, chicken or turkey.

Souffleéd Baby Clams

Serves 6 people

8 oz (225 g) tinned baby
   clams, drained weight
grated rind of ½ lemon
1 teaspoon lemon juice
3–4 tablespoons good
   mayonnaise
salt and pepper, to taste
Tabasco (optional)
8 large slices wholemeal
   bread
3 egg whites

Combine the drained baby clams with the lemon rind, juice and mayonnaise. Add salt and pepper and a dash of Tabasco if you like a tongue-tingle with seafood. Leave the mixture in a cool, but not refrigerated, place.

Cut the crusts off the bread and cut each slice into 6 or 9 pieces, depending on how dainty you feel. Toast one side only under a grill. At this stage, you can leave everything until just a few minutes before you are ready to serve.

Then, turn the grill to a moderate heat. Whip the egg whites until stiff, but not dry, and fold them into the clam mixture. Mound high on the untoasted sides of the bread and arrange these on a baking tray or attractive oven dish.

Put under the grill until puffed and brown, but don't take your eyes off them, as they only take about 45 seconds. Serve immediately. Remember to have extra paper napkins around, if guests are going to eat them in their fingers as a pre-meal snack with drinks.

Asparagus Pastries with Maltese Sauce

Serves 6 people

1½ lb (700 g) thin asparagus, trimmed weight
1½ lb (700 g) puff pastry (but you can be more generous)
1 egg yolk, for glazing

Maltese Sauce
1 dessertspoon tarragon vinegar
2 dessertspoons water
yolks of 2 very fresh eggs
8 oz (225 g) butter, melted
finely grated rind of 1 orange
orange juice, if required

Pre-heat the oven to 200°C/400°F/Gas 6.

Reserve 4 oz (110 g) of the pastry, and roll the rest out into a rectangle roughly 15″ × 10″ (37.5 cm × 25 cm). Trim it neatly and cut into 6 even pieces, approximately 6″ (15 cm) long and 3″ (7.5 cm) wide.

Roll out the remaining 4 oz (110 g) pastry and cut 12 narrow strips from it measuring about 8″ (20 cm) in length. Twist each of these a couple of times and secure with a touch of egg yolk along the long sides only of each larger rectangle of pastry, two per rectangle.

Paint each pastry shape with the egg yolk and bake on an oven tray until well risen, crisp and golden brown (about 15–20 minutes). If you are making them earlier than you need them, reduce the temperature of the oven after 15 minutes to the lowest possible setting and leave to thoroughly dry out (otherwise they become soggy), for another 30 minutes.

Choose only thin asparagus and trim the bottoms of each spear until they are slightly longer than the cooked pastry shapes. Poach the spears in slightly salted water, keeping them crisp and very green. I always do this in shallow water in a large frying pan so the spears do not lie on top of one

STARTERS AND SOUPS

another. Drain and cover with clingfilm until it is time to serve.

Meanwhile make the Maltese Sauce, which is an orange-flavoured hollandaise, the ultimate sauce for asparagus. It should be made with blood oranges, but others do nicely. Don't be afraid of making hollandaise. You need only a food processor or muscle to succeed.

Combine the tarragon vinegar and one spoonful of water in a small pan and reduce over heat by three-quarters. Turn down the heat as far as you can. Add the rest of the water and the 2 egg yolks. Stir continuously with a wooden spoon until they begin to thicken, but take care not to let them scramble.

Now beat in the melted butter, which should be warm and not hot. If you have a food processor or a blender, it takes seconds; if you don't, it takes ages.

Add the orange rind and some orange juice if you'd like more of that flavour. You may also like to reduce more tarragon vinegar and add a drop or two of that to sharpen the sauce. Place some clingfilm over the surface of the sauce and leave at room temperature – in my experience it's happy for 4 to 5 hours.

To assemble and serve, re-heat the pastries gently in the oven. Pour boiling water over the asparagus and leave 30 seconds. Drain well. Arrange the hot asparagus in the pastries, all lying the same way, then spoon the sauce across them in strips. Avoid pouring the sauce *along* the asparagus as you will lose the colour contrast.

If you are really rushed, these pastries can be prepared well in advance and eaten at room temperature. The difference between hot and cold is not grave.

---

*As much as I love asparagus I hate the fuss of fingerbowls. I created these pastries as a way to eat asparagus with a knife and fork, and served on white plates, they look and taste wonderful.

The left-over egg whites can be used to make the next recipe.

Salmon Soufflé in Artichokes

Serves 6

6 large globe artichokes
1 lemon
1 tablespoon oil
1 oz (30 g) butter
1 tablespoon plain flour
¼ pint (150 ml) warm milk
½ teaspoon dried tarragon
2 dessertspoons Parmesan cheese, grated

salt, pepper
8 oz (225 g) tinned pink salmon, crushed, skin and bones removed
3 egg yolks
4 egg whites

First prepare the artichokes. Slice off the stalk and the top third of the artichokes with a very sharp knife and quickly rub the cut edges with lemon. Spread the middle leaves and with a strong teaspoon, excavate the hairy choke and most of the central purple leaves. Squirt the exposed heart with more juice from the lemon. Wash well.

Cook the artichokes in lots of boiling salted water with some more of the lemon juice plus the tablespoon of oil. They should be tender in 20 minutes; check by poking a fork gently into the bottom. It should slide through easily. Drain well, inverted.

To make the soufflé, first pre-heat the oven to 180°C/350°F/Gas 4. Melt the butter in a small saucepan, add the flour and cook gently for a few minutes. Slowly add the milk, and whisk all together. Add the tarragon and cheese, then season well with salt and pepper. Cook for a few minutes more, and then take off the heat.

Stir in the liquid from the salmon plus the mashed flesh. Beat in the egg yolks. Whip the egg whites until stiff but not dry and fold into the salmon mixture. Spoon evenly into the artichokes. Place on a baking tray and cook for 25 minutes.

STARTERS AND SOUPS

Pink Cloud Pâté

Serves 6–8 people

½ lb (225 g) prawns, shelled
3 oz (85 g) warm, melted butter
juice of 1 lemon
2 oz (60 g) cottage cheese

⅛ pint (75 ml) double cream
brandy or white vermouth
4 oz (110 g) butter, melted, for sealing
dill weed for decoration

As the prawns are probably frozen, defrost them slowly in the refrigerator. This produces a much better flavour and texture than when you defrost at room temperature or, worse, help them along with hot or cold water.

Using a food processor or blender make a purée of the prawns, adding the 3 oz (85 g) melted butter and the lemon juice. You may choose also to add a little white pepper; I don't.

Turn the purée into a bowl and allow to cool, until it is just about to set. Beat or sieve the cottage cheese to remove all the lumps; whip the cream and fold into the cheese. Fold the cheese and cream mixture into the prawn purée and finish with about a capful of brandy, or of white vermouth – an interesting alternative.

Put into individual ramekins or a pretty plain white bowl or dish. Seal with a little melted, but cool, butter (the quantity depends on what kind and what size of dish). Sprinkle some chopped dill on top.

*You can use this recipe as the basis for other seafood pâtés and can double it for parties. Infinitely superior to cooked fish pâtés, as the original fish flavour is discernible, and the texture is wonderful. Serve it with little arcs of seeded, poached cucumber, which gleam like jade when cold.

You can omit the cottage cheese and use ¼ pint (150 ml) double cream instead.

STARTERS AND SOUPS

Green Peppercorn Tuna

Serves 6–8 people

1½ lb (700 g) fresh or frozen tuna, cleaned weight
6–8 fresh limes
1 small tin green peppercorns in brine
¼ pint (150 ml) white wine
bunch of green coriander or parsley

Beg your fishmonger to clean and fillet the tuna which you will easily recognise as it resembles a larger, fatter, unstriped mackerel. If he doesn't oblige, ask for advice and do it yourself.

Then cut each fillet into four pieces by making one lengthwise and one crosswise cut. Trim and skin, then cut each piece into very thin slices along its length. You'll need patience and a sharp knife, and if the fish is still slightly frozen, so much the better.

Arrange a first layer of these slices in an earthenware dish. Squeeze some fresh lime juice over them, then sprinkle with some brine from the peppercorns. Crush six peppercorns and distribute them, followed by some roughly chopped coriander or parsley. Continue thus until all the fish is used. Place alternate layers at right angles to each other so the marinade can penetrate easily. Pour in white wine so that the marinade just covers the fish. Cover and refrigerate for at least 10 hours.

Drain off the marinade and arrange the tuna slices on a chilled platter or individual serving plates. Decorate only with coriander or parsley, and a thin slice of lime if you have any left over, and serve with brown bread and butter.

*Green coriander, with its bitter yet fascinating flavour, is usually found in Greek, Turkish or Arab shops, but it is

STARTERS AND SOUPS

certainly a taste which many will never acquire.

Other oily fish might be substituted for the tuna, such as mackerel, but it must be so fresh you can still smell the sea on it. At the opposite end of the fish scale (so to speak), salmon also reacts wonderfully to such treatment. Speaking of which, the next recipe, for pickled salmon, clearly demonstrates the visual difference between marinating and pickling of fish; in the former the flesh becomes opaque while in the latter the flesh remains translucent.

Green Peppercorn Tuna is always a sensation when I serve it at a buffet. I usually make the following variation as well. Having sliced the tuna as above, I marinate the slices in lemon and orange juice (2 lemons to 4 oranges) and arrange very thin slices of fresh green ginger root between the layers. Top up with white wine if necessary.

Pickled Salmon with Green Ginger Mayonnaise

Serves 6 people, twice over

1 fresh salmon or sea-trout weighing 5–6 lb (2.3–2.7 kg)
3 oz (85 g) white sugar
3 oz (85 g) salt
20 white peppercorns, coarsely crushed
plenty of fresh dill weed
½ pint (300 ml) mayonnaise
a piece of green ginger root approximately 1" × 1½" (2.5 cm × 4 cm), peeled

Scale and clean the fish. Remove the head and tail, and wipe with a damp towel (do not wash). Remove each side of the fish in one slice. Using a pair of pliers with pointed and serrated ends (or a similar tweezer), remove the remaining bones which pierce the flesh from the cavity side towards the skin. It is really worthwhile being painstaking about this.

Mix the sugar and salt together and add the crushed peppercorns.

In a deep earthenware or glass dish in which the salmon can lie flat, make a bed of about one quarter of the fresh dill. Scatter this with a quarter of the sugar, salt and peppercorn pickling mixture. Put one side of fish on this, skin side down, and rub another quarter of the pickle into the flesh. Cover with another quarter of the dill. Put pickle mix and dill on the flesh of the other piece of fish and lay it on the first, flesh to flesh, but head to tail. Sprinkle with the last of the pickle and the dill – you cannot be too generous. Put a board or another plate on top of the fish and weight down with tins. In a cool cellar, the pickle needs only 24 hours; in a colder refrigerator, it needs 48 hours. Turn the fish every 6 hours or so.

To prepare for serving, scrape the dill and peppercorns off one side and lie it skin down on a cutting board. Slice very thinly towards the tail, angling slightly downwards, so that soon each slice finishes on the skin with no flesh is wasted.

In Sweden, this dish is called Gravad Lax and is served with a mustardy sauce which I personally think clashes with the dill and salmon flavours. I suggest you chop some of the pickled dill and add it to the ½ pint (300 ml) of excellent mayonnaise. Flavour this with the juice of green ginger, by crushing pieces of the ginger in a garlic press over the mayonnaise.

For very special occasions, poach some very special eggs to the point where the white is firm but the yolks are runny. Put one or two of these, according to size, on each serving and slit the yolks. If these eggs were to be those of the quail, pheasant, gull or pullet, and if they were also to sit in a nest of the green ginger mayonnaise, I think you would be well pleased.

*I know salmon is very expensive, and sea-trout only marginally less so, but most of us have celebratory occasions when some expense can be justified and afforded. The remaining side of the fish will last for a week at least in the refrigerator.

If you have access to plenty of salmon, I suggest you try pickling it with a herb other than dill – try mint, tarragon, lemon balm or parsley. Then let me know what it tastes like. But don't be tempted to include anything acidic, like onion or citrus juice, for these will turn the flesh opaque, whereas it should glow and be transparent on the plate.

Coronet of Smoked Oysters

Serves 6 people

4 oz (110 g) tin smoked oysters
1 lb (450 g) Jerusalem artichokes
1 chicken stock cube
1 large clove garlic
salt
5 drops Tabasco
¾ pint (430 ml) tomato juice
juice of 1 large lemon
1 dessertspoon chopped parsley
¼ pint (150 ml) double cream, lightly whipped
¾ oz (25 g) gelatine (1½ packets)

Chill an oiled 2 pint (1.2 litre) ring mould or soufflé dish.

Drain the smoked oysters, reserving the oil and juice. Peel the artichokes (there is no choice this time). Cut them into small pieces and cook just covered with water to which you have added the liquid from the oysters, the stock cube, garlic, salt and Tabasco. When just tender, take off the heat, and purée everything together with the cooking liquid and strain through a fine sieve. You should have ¾ pint (430 ml) of purée. If not, reduce carefully or add milk. Add ½ pint (300 ml) *only* of the tomato juice. Leave to cool.

Cut the oysters in half, drench with lemon juice, toss in the parsley and arrange at the bottom of the mould. Spread the lightly-whipped cream evenly over them.

Now melt the gelatine in the remaining tomato juice over a gentle heat. Strain and carefully stir into the artichoke mixture.

Pour enough of the artichoke mixture into the mould to cover the cream on top of the oysters. Stir gently to create a marbled effect with the cream. Put the mould into the refrigerator to allow the mixture to set firmly.

Then pour in the rest of the mixture and leave to chill thoroughly and set, in the refrigerator, for at least 4 hours.

Turn out to serve, with extra parsley and some brown bread.

STARTERS AND SOUPS

Virginian Prawns

Serves 2 people

8 oz (225 g) large prawns, peeled
4 rashers smoked streaky bacon
2 oz (60 g) butter (but be generous)
6 tablespoons dry white wine
1 clove garlic, crushed
½ small onion, very finely chopped
½ pint (300 ml) double cream
5 teaspoons creamed horseradish

Cut the bacon into small dice and fry gently in a small uncovered pan until the fat has run and the pieces are a light gold. Remove the bacon and keep warm.

Into the bacon fat put the butter, wine, garlic and onion. Cook gently until the onion is soft and translucent. Pour in the double cream, stir well, then leave to simmer gently until reduced by half. It should be a thick, coating consistency. For the sake of appearance, I would strain out the onion now, but it's not strictly necessary.

Flavour the sauce with horseradish. Be careful to taste as you proceed as different horseradish creams or sauces vary enormously in pungency. If you do make the sauce too hot, cook it a little longer and the tang will diminish.

Add the prawns and heat through. Don't boil or keep warm too long or the prawns will either toughen or dilute the sauce too much. Serve over rice, sprinkled with the bacon bits.

*This recipe is based on a dinner I ate at the Red Fox Inn at Middleburg, Virginia, long before it was discovered by Elizabeth Taylor. . . .

STARTERS AND SOUPS

Stuffed Kidney Cushions

Serves 6 people

6 whole lamb kidneys
1 dessertspoon butter
4 oz (110 g) mushrooms,
 finely chopped
2 dessertspoons dry sherry or
 brandy
2 teaspoons Dijon or other
 strong mustard
1 clove garlic, crushed
1 teaspoon dried oregano
1 rounded dessertspoon dry,
 white breadcrumbs
salt and pepper
¾ lb (340 g) puff pastry
1 egg yolk, for glazing

Using kitchen scissors, cut the fat from each kidney. Remove the outer membrane. With a sharp knife, deepen the pocket from which you have removed the fat; go as far as you can without piercing the kidney.

In a small saucepan put the butter, mushrooms, alcohol, mustard, garlic and oregano. Cook for a few minutes over a medium heat until the juices of the mushrooms are flowing, stir in the breadcrumbs, remove from heat, and add salt and pepper to taste. Let cool.

If you can only buy small packets of frozen pastry (usually about ½ lb or 225 g) one of these will be perfectly adequate, but the larger amount of pastry gives more spectacular results.

STARTERS AND SOUPS

Pre-heat the oven to 230°C/450°F/Gas 8. Divide the pastry into six pieces and roll into rectangles twice as long and twice as wide as each kidney. Trim the edges neatly and leave the pastry to relax.

Stuff the kidneys with the cooled mushroom mixture. Then place each kidney, stuffing uppermost, lengthwise on a piece of pastry. Wet the pastry borders, then fold up to the kidney, short sides first, long sides second. The pastry cushion should cover the kidney, but leave the stuffing uncovered. Pinch the edges together to hold in place. Paint the pastry with egg yolk, and place the cushions on a baking tray. Cook for 25 minutes or longer if you don't like pink kidneys.

You could also serve these cushions as a light supper, accompanied by extra mustard, a good salad, and hot garlic bread.

STARTERS AND SOUPS

Leeks with Gremolata

For each person, select two thin leeks or one medium leek. Trim and clean the leeks very well, cook them briefly in salted water and drain. Press lightly between kitchen paper towels to extract the last of the water. While still warm, bathe in a dressing made with olive oil and lemon juice, then leave in the refrigerator, covered, to chill thoroughly – at least 4 hours.

Gremolata is a mixture of chopped parsley, lemon peel and garlic, found properly as the garnish for Osso Buco, that wonderful Italian casserole of veal shin. It's terrific as a taste-booster to many things, including grilled or pan-fried liver. But back to leeks.

For each serving, chop enough parsley to fill a dessertspoon then add a teaspoon of chopped lemon peel and half a small clove of garlic, finely chopped. Sprinkle over the leeks and serve.

Leeks Aux Noix

Prepare the leeks as above, but make the dressing with walnut oil instead of olive, and serve with a scattering of chopped walnuts. More intriguingly, you can make a gremolata for the leeks and chop walnuts into it.

*Walnut oil will change your life. It has an extraordinary affinity with tomatoes; in fact eat them just with oil and nothing else. Its rich bite and subtle nutty flavour is tremendous with endive and orange salad, in casseroles – anything in which oil is used. It is expensive and it also goes rancid very easily. It should be kept in a cool and dark place, preferably the refrigerator.

Main Courses and Sauces

MAIN COURSES

Saffron Seafood Millefeuille

Serves 6 people

12 oz (340 g) phyllo pastry sheets *or* 1 lb (450 g) puff pastry
12 oz (340 g) leeks, sliced thinly
½ pint (300 ml) milk
1 oz (30 g) butter
1 oz (30 g) flour
salt, freshly ground white pepper
2 sachets powdered saffron
12 oz (340 g) mixed pre-cooked seafood, including shellfish (*see method*)

Pre-heat oven to 200°C/400°F/Gas 6.

If you are lucky enough to find phyllo pastry, cut the sheets in half (across the length) and trim all around with a very sharp knife. Make two piles of the sheets, painting each sheet with melted butter as instructed on the packaging. With a sharp knife or razor blade, make a diamond pattern by cutting through the top layers of just one of the piles of phyllo. Bake both piles on an oiled baking sheet until crisp, curled and golden brown all through, painting with water if the edges curl or burn before this stage. Remove to cool or keep warm in the oven if you are proceeding immediately.

If you only have puff pastry, roll it out to two oblongs about 12 × 8″ (30 × 20 cm). Scallop the edges of one piece and paint that with an egg yolk. Bake both until well risen, brown and thoroughly dried throughout. Reserve as above.

The thinly sliced leeks should include a good amount of the green and be thoroughly washed and drained. Put them into the cold milk, bring very slowly to the boil, and cook until they just begin to wilt, but still retain their brilliant colour.

Drain, reserving both the leeks and the milk. Use this hot flavoured milk to make the béchamel. Melt the butter in a small saucepan, add the flour and cook for 1–2 minutes. Let cool for a minute, then strain in the hot leeky milk and stir well together. Bring to the boil, stirring continually, and simmer for 3 minutes. Add the saffron to the béchamel and simmer very gently for 10 minutes or so to bring out the flavour. This sauce can be prepared in advance and left with a butter paper over it.

Meanwhile, prepare your seafood, which can be a single variety or a mixture. Large prawns or scampi are good by themselves, so are scallops or mussels. Personally I like a good mixture and if you are using some of the very good tinned shellfish (Danish mussels are excellent), add their liquid to the saffron sauce. Add the seafood to the sauce, and heat gently (fierce heat or boiling will toughen most fish).

The final assembly can and should be done at the last minute. While the seafood is heating gently in the sauce, re-heat the pastry. The leeks can be re-heated by tossing them in butter or pouring boiling water over them, leaving for 30 seconds, and draining well. Put the plain layer of pastry on a heated platter, and distribute the leeks evenly over it. Then pour over the saffron seafood sauce and top that with the decorated pastry. Cut into portions at the table with a long sharp knife.

*I invented this for Mary Crowley of Sausalito, who found me the ship on which I sailed to Pitcairn Island in summer 1980. Innumerable letters from her friends begging for the recipe are adequate testimony to its breathtaking appearance and flavour. I often use crisply cooked leeks as the base for seafood or chicken dishes which have a sauce; far prettier, easier in the kitchen – and no starch!

Once you find a Greek shop that sells phyllo, buy a stock and freeze it. Even the best puff pastry can't equal its fly-away effect.

Holiday Pie

Serves 6 people

12 oz (340 g) puff pastry
½ lb (225 g) bacon (smoked streaky is best)
6 large eggs
salt and pepper

Pre-heat oven to 200°C/400°F/Gas 6.
 Line an 8–9" (20–22.5 cm) pie dish with half the pastry. Coarsely dice the bacon and fry until the fat starts to run. Drain, then spread the pieces evenly over the pastry. Break the eggs over the bacon, arranging five around the edge and one in the middle. Encourage the whites to join up, but try not to break the yolks. Sprinkle each egg yolk with a pinch of salt and grind black pepper over the lot.
 Cover with the rest of the pastry. Decorate if you wish, then bake for 25 minutes. Lower the temperature to 170°C/325°F/Gas 3 for a further 15 minutes. Serve hot or cold.

*This recipe from New Zealand is far more practical for picnics than the dreaded, omnipresent, soggy quiche; it tastes better than most too. The addition of a few strongly-flavoured extras changes what is essentially a bacon-and-egg pie into something special. Diced green pepper, green peas, onion or fried potato are the best. Sprinkle them on to the bacon before you add the eggs. . . . Pretty beaut, as we say Down Under.

Moselle Chicken

Serves 8–10 people

1 lb (450 g) chicken meat
1 sachet aspic
scant 1 pint (½ litre) Moselle
  wine
6 oz (170 g) seedless white
  grapes
1 bulb fennel with plenty of
  green frond

One pound (450 g) weight is approximately the amount of meat you would expect to retrieve from an oven-ready bird weighing 2½ lb (1.12 kg). When I made this, I steamed the whole chicken in a tightly-fitting casserole with a lemon, squeezed of its juice and cut into chunks. I cooled it on its breast to keep it moist, then flaked it by hand into large pieces, as evenly shaped as possible. But you could use the flesh from a bought, ready-cooked chicken.

Melt the aspic powder in half the wine over a gentle heat for about 3 minutes, then add the other half and allow to cool.

Meanwhile, lightly oil a 3 pint (1.7 litre) mould. Put some of the grapes at the bottom and cover with fronds of fennel, layering some up the sides of the mould. Dribble on a little of the aspic and leave to set.

Slice or chop the fennel neatly. Either mix together the fennel, grapes and chicken meat and put into the mould, or add them in neat layers. They should almost fill the mould. Spoon in the cooled aspic, then cover the top with more fennel fronds. Chill for 6–8 hours.

Unmould and serve in thin slices, cut with an extremely sharp knife. It's very good with the Spiced Peaches on page 48. Sour cream with horseradish added is also excellent and suitably Germanic.

Herby Chicken

Serves 6 people

- 6 chicken breasts on the bone *or* 6 chicken suprêmes
- 1 oz (30 g) butter
- 1 tablespoon oil
- 2 big handfuls parsley
- 1 small bunch fresh thyme
- 1 small bunch fresh mint
- 4 small sprigs fresh rosemary
- scattering of other sweet herbs, such as basil, lemon balm, marjoram etc
- $\frac{1}{8}$ pint (75 ml) water or white wine

Remove the wings and skin from the breasts; these are exceptionally good roasted or fried with absolutely masses of chopped garlic. Heat a knob of butter and a little oil in a heavy pan and fry the breasts until just beginning to show a nice golden colour. If you have walnut oil, this will give the best flavour by far.

Pre-heat the oven to 220°C/425°F/Gas 7.

Mix the herbs together. Rinse in cold water and drain but do not shake; divide into 3 piles. Place an even layer of herbs on the bottom of a heavy casserole with a tight-fitting lid, and arrange three breasts (if still on the bone, flesh side down) on top. Evenly layer the second pile of herbs, then the remaining three breasts, then the last of the herbs.

Pour into the casserole any pan juices left over from browning the chicken plus the water or white wine. Put foil over the casserole and fit the lid tightly over that. Cook in oven for 20 minutes then reduce heat to 180°C/350°F/Gas 4 for another 25 minutes.

Two minutes before you want to serve the chicken, open the casserole and carefully pour off most of the herb-flavoured juices; reduce vigorously. Serve each breast on a bed of white or brown rice and spoon the reduced sauce over the top. (Any remaining juice or sauce makes an excellent addition to soup or stock.)

*Whatever herbs you use, you must have the large quantity of parsley indicated, as this acts as a balance for the other flavours. If you have used walnut oil, you might like to enhance its flavour by also serving Tomato and Walnut Sauce (page 49), although this would add a considerable number of calories.

Jubilee Poultry

Cold chicken or turkey in a curry-flavoured mayonnaise was once called Coronation Chicken. Then it became Jubilee Chicken. And I heard it recently called Royal Wedding Chicken. Royalist or not, it remains a good way to serve cold poultry, despite it being served at ninety per cent of the buffets catered for by Girl Fridays.

There is no real recipe. But for about 1 lb (450 g) of flaked poultry, you will need something like ½ pint (300 ml) mayonnaise. To that add a dessertspoon curry powder or curry paste, which you have warmed through (to encourage full development of the flavours). Then stir in 2 tablespoons mango chutney and sharpen the mixture with a squeeze or two of lemon juice. Mix everything gently and well together and leave to chill for several hours in a refrigerator.

If you like more exact instructions, follow the next recipe, omitting the fruit.

Serve Jubilee Poultry with a rice salad or a green salad, accompanied by Spiced Peaches (page 48).

Peachy Chicken

Serves 4–6 people for lunch

1–1½ lb (450–700 g) chicken meat, flaked
¾ pint (400 ml) excellent mayonnaise
4 teaspoons curry powder
6 oz (170 g) peach chutney
2 fresh peaches, sliced

Check that the mayonnaise has a good clean taste; if it is in the least heavy, add a little lemon juice or tarragon vinegar.

Warm the curry powder slightly and mix lightly into the mayonnaise. Stir in the chicken pieces and the peach chutney, trying not to break up any large pieces.

Plunge the fresh peaches into boiling water for 1 minute, then peel and cut into even slices. Fold very gently into the mixture.

Chill in the refrigerator for 4 hours and then serve with rice cooked with bay leaves, sprinkled with chopped, toasted hazelnuts or almonds, if you like. For extra elegance, add some whipped cream to the mayonnaise, thus making a mousseline.

Turkey with Tarragon Pears

Serves 6–8 people, more at a buffet

1½–2 lb (700–900 g) cold
   turkey, flaked
1 lb (450 g) ripe, sweet pears
¼ pint (150 ml) tarragon
   vinegar
1 pint (600 ml) mayonnaise
2 cloves garlic

Peel and core the pears, slice them neatly and put into the tarragon vinegar; turn a few times to ensure an even coating which will prevent discoloration. If you have no tarragon vinegar, heat 1 tablespoon of dried tarragon in ¼ pint (150 ml) of white wine in a covered pan until just starting to simmer. Remove from heat, cool and drain.

Prepare the turkey flesh, discarding any skin or gristle. The finished dish will look more appealing and less like leftovers if you make the flakes of turkey even and generous, rather than ragged and puny.

Drain the pears, reserving the vinegar. Stir 2 tablespoons of the vinegar into the mayonnaise and squeeze in the juice of the garlic with a garlic press. Gently fold the turkey and pears into the mayonnaise. Leave in a cool place for 2 hours or 4 hours in the refrigerator. This gives time for the flavours to intermingle – which is most important. Taste, and add more vinegar if you would like a more pronounced flavour.

Serve in a ring of chilled rice cooked with lots of bay leaf. If you have such fresh herbs as tarragon, basil, thyme, lemon balm or parsley, chop some roughly and scatter over the top.

*You can make this with chicken too, but as you are more likely to have only 1 lb (450 g) of chicken meat, halve the other ingredients.

MAIN COURSES

Beef Fillet with Mango

Serves 4 people

1–1½ lb (450–700 g) beef
 fillet, trimmed
2 medium, firm mangoes
2 large cloves garlic
1" (2.5 cm) piece green ginger
 root, peeled
1 dessertspoon oil
2 dessertspoons oyster sauce

Cut both the beef and the peeled mangoes, separately, into strips about 2 × ½" (5 × 1.25 cm). Finely chop and mix together the garlic and ginger. Lightly coat a heavy frying pan with oil and sauté the garlic and ginger until *just* starting to turn colour. Add the beef, and now stir constantly until all pieces are sealed. Sprinkle in the oyster sauce and distribute evenly. Gently fold in the mangoes, trying hard to keep the pieces in shape.

When heated through, serve immediately on a bed of plain rice and with one perfectly cooked green vegetable – some broccoli spears, perhaps, scattered with chopped almonds, or some mangetouts.

*I've adapted this recipe from one served at Tiger Lee in London, the only Oriental restaurant in Europe with a Michelin star. It's actually a Cantonese seafood restaurant, where most things you choose to eat are alive and swimming when you first come through the door. Why give a beef recipe from a seafood restaurant? I've been wondering myself. Perhaps because I've only been able to afford to make this once, and want to savour the idea again. The combination of garlic and green ginger is found throughout the East.

Rabbit with Gin and Juniper

Serves 4 people

1 jointed rabbit *or* 1½ lb (700 g) boneless rabbit meat
¼ lb (110 g) smoked, streaky bacon, cut into strips
1 dessertspoon oil
1 large onion, sliced
1 clove garlic, chopped
1 bay leaf
½ small lemon, cut into chunks
¼ pint (150 ml) gin
⅛ pint (75 ml) water
12 juniper berries, crushed
1 teaspoon salt
¼ pint (150 ml) sour cream

Pre-heat oven to 110°C/225°F/Gas ¼.

Gently fry the bacon in a little oil. When the fat is running freely, add the onion and garlic and cook until soft and transparent, but not brown.

Seal the rabbit meat in the fat and onions, but try not to brown it. Add the bay, lemon, gin, water, juniper berries, and the salt. Put into a casserole, place in the oven, and cook for 3 hours.

Before serving, remove the bay and the lemon. Stir a few spoonfuls of the stock into the sour cream and beat to remove the lumps. Blend the sour cream into the casserole liquid and reheat without boiling.

You need lots of buttered rice with this. Parsnip chips, grilled tomatoes and crisp green beans are other good accompaniments.

Spirited Pheasant

Serves 4–6 people

2 pheasants, plucked and drawn
3 large cloves garlic
2 teaspoons green peppercorns
¼ lb (110 g) butter, at room temperature
1 oz (30 g) walnuts, shelled
⅛ pint (75 ml) whisky, Drambuie, orange liqueur or brandy

Wipe the birds with a damp cloth but do not, repeat, do not wash them. Place in a roasting pan.

Put the garlic, peppercorns and butter into a food processor and mix well. Add the walnuts slowly, processing just until the butter starts to clump together, but some of the walnuts are still in big pieces. No processor? Chop the garlic, peppercorns and walnuts with a heavy knife and mash them into the butter.

Heat your chosen spirit in a small saucepan. Ignite and pour over the birds. Agitate the pan to maintain the flames as long as possible. Smear half the prepared butter over the birds' breasts and leave in a cool place for at least 2 hours, 5 hours at the most.

Pre-heat the oven to 220°C/425°F/Gas 7.

Turn the birds on their side. Cover the pan with foil and roast for 15 minutes. Turn the birds onto their other side, baste, then cover again and roast for a further 15 minutes. Remove the foil, baste very well and lay the birds on their back. Smear on the remaining butter and roast 15 minutes more, covering the breasts loosely with foil if the nuts start to burn.

Remove the pan from the oven and pour off the pan juices. Turn the birds onto their breasts and leave for 10 minutes while you finish the sauce. Simply reduce the pan juices over heat by half with a little extra of the spirit you used, if you think that would be good.

Either carve the birds, or more simply cut each in half with kitchen scissors. I dislike the traditional accompaniments for game – chips and sweet jellies and so on. Try serving spiced red cabbage and a purée of celeriac, rich with butter and coloured with chopped parsley. They are elegant and make a more substantial meal. If you can't buy celeriac, creamy mashed potatoes, again with parsley, are always far more appreciated than those thin chips, which you can neither spear nor coax on to your fork.

*Remembering always to cook birds on their sides ensures succulence. For small birds it is essential. When I cook grouse, for instance, I turn them from side to side and then on to their breasts, never allowing the juices to run into the body cavity and be wasted. All birds, even turkeys, should rest on their breasts for some time after being removed from the oven. Although it may put them slightly out of shape, they will be much juicier.

Three-Way Spiced Mackerel

Each variation serves 4 people

4 medium mackerel

Recipe 1
½ pint (300 ml) cider or garlic vinegar
2 teaspoons pickling spice
1 bay leaf
½ onion, sliced

Recipe 2
½ pint (300 ml) cider
2 teaspoons pickling spice
1 clove garlic, crushed
1 onion, sliced
1 cooking apple, cut into thick slices

Recipe 3
½ pint (300 ml) red wine
2 bay leaves
1 onion, sliced
12 whole allspice berries
1 lemon, sliced
½ orange, sliced

Turn your oven to its lowest heat.

Put the cleaned fish into an earthenware dish which will hold them all flat without touching one another. Add all the marinade ingredients of whichever recipe you have chosen. Cover with foil and bake 4 hours.

To serve the fish hot, remove the fish from the liquid with a slotted spoon or fish slice and return them, covered, to the oven. Reduce the liquid in a pan rapidly over heat until it is slightly thick, and then strain. If you would like it richer, beat in a few teaspoons of butter. Arrange the fish on a platter and pour the sauce over them.

To serve cold, simply remove the baking dish from the oven, let cool and remove the spices, onion etc. Refrigerate the fish overnight in the liquid, which will turn into jelly. Serve each fish with some of this jelly, chopped up. Recipe 2 can be served with some hot or cold apple sauce, lightly flavoured with cinnamon; Recipe 3 appreciates the same sauce, but with the addition of a little grated orange peel.

Baked Aubergine Noodles

Serves 4–6 people

2 lb (900 g) aubergines
12 oz (340 g) spinach noodles
   (*tagliatelle*), dry weight
2 oz (60 g) butter
14 oz (400 g) tin plum
   tomatoes
3 large cloves garlic
1 teaspoon ground coriander
1 teaspoon ground cumin
½ teaspoon cayenne pepper
4 tablespoons oil, at least
salt, pepper, lemon juice

Slice the aubergines thickly, leaving the skin on (you get a nicer effect if you cut diagonally). Sprinkle lavishly with salt and leave to drain in a colander for at least 1 hour; turn from time to time. Rinse under cold water, drain and pat dry.

Meanwhile, cook the pasta in lots of salted water until *al dente*. Drain and toss in the butter. Add the spices to the tomatoes and their juice, and simmer uncovered in a small saucepan for 20 minutes.

Pre-heat oven to 180°C/350°F/Gas 4.

Fry the aubergine slices in oil until starting to soften (they will *really* soak up the oil), drain and dry on paper towels. Divide the cooked aubergine into three piles.

To assemble, put a layer of aubergine at the bottom of a deep casserole, and sprinkle with salt, pepper and a third of the tomato sauce. Add half the pasta. Repeat aubergine layer, seasoning and a third of the tomato. Put the remaining pasta on top, and finish with the third aubergine layer, covered with the rest of the sauce. Bake, covered, for 45 minutes.

MAIN COURSES

Capelletti with Salmon Filling

Serves 4 people

8 oz (225 g) strong, white
 (bread) flour
2 eggs
4 teaspoons olive oil

Salmon filling
6 oz (170 g) tin pink salmon
2 dessertspoons Parmesan
 cheese, grated
½ teaspoon dried tarragon
½ teaspoon ground nutmeg

Capelletti are a little-known shape of pasta, rather like tortellini. So first you need to make some pasta. Put the flour onto a board, and make a well in the middle. Break the eggs into the well, mix together with your hands, and knead until silky and smooth. You can add a little water if you think it necessary. Cover the dough with a damp cloth and rest 10 minutes.

Divide the dough into four pieces, for convenience, then roll each one out as thinly as possible, using plenty of flour on the board and on your rolling pin.

Leave to dry for 10 minutes, and while it's drying, make the filling. Mix all the ingredients together with some of the juice from the salmon, to make a smooth paste.

To make the Capelletti, cut the rolled, dried dough into 1–1½″ (2.5–3.75 cm) squares. Dot the filling in the middle of each. Fold over one corner so that it just covers the filling, then fold over that fold again. Seal, then turn around your finger and pinch the ends together. You should have a circle of stuffed pasta with a small triangle pointing from one side, looking like a headscarf (which is why Bob Holness and I call these Sloane Rangers).

Cook your stuffed capelletti in masses of boiling salted water for a few minutes, or just until they float to the surface. Remove with a slotted spoon and serve with melted butter, seasoned with lemon juice. Sprinkle over any salmon you have left. It almost goes without saying that a squeeze of garlic juice in that buttery sauce would not go amiss.

*Capelletti can also be filled with curd or ricotta cheese mixed with nutmeg and a little chopped spinach, or with bolognese sauce (page 50).

This basic recipe for pasta can also be used for other pasta shapes. For simple noodles, for instance, just roll up the rolled, dried dough like a sponge roll and cut through into thin slices with a very sharp knife. Fresh pasta takes only a few minutes to cook. It should never be drained or put into sauce; you should spoon it out of the water onto a plate, where it will dry itself in seconds. Then the sauce should be poured over and around it, and mixed in at the moment of serving. Or it should be served onto individual plates and the sauce handed round separately.

MAIN COURSES

Beef Paprikas

Serves 4 people

2 lb (900 g) chuck steak, cut
   into large chunks
½ lb (225 g) onions, very finely sliced
1 tablespoon oil
seasoned flour
1 × 14–16 oz (400–450 g) tin
   plum tomatoes
3 heaped teaspoons sweet paprika
2 heaped teaspoons hot paprika
¼ pint (150 ml) soured cream

Soften, but do not brown the onions in the oil. Turn the meat in seasoned flour and seal in the hot oil and onions. Add the tomatoes. Mix together the two paprikas and add half the amount to the saucepan.

Cook, covered, over low heat until the meat is very tender and the sauce has developed a pleasing consistency. If it is too thin, tilt or remove the lid to allow faster evaporation. A few minutes before serving, stir in the remaining paprika and the sour cream. Mix well and serve with plainly cooked, mealy potatoes.

*This authentic Hungarian recipe is what most people would think of as goulash; it isn't. You may also make it with pork or chicken.

Sweet paprika can sometimes be used by itself, but this is not usually the practice in countries which feature paprika in their national dishes. Usually, each household mixes an individual balance of sweet and hot paprika. *Always* use a mixture, making it hotter or sweeter according to the food. Hungarian paprika is the hot one, Spanish is sweet.

Kleftiko Cleopatra

Serves 4–6 people

1 shoulder of lamb, cut into
   4–6 pieces
juice of 1 lemon
⅛ pint (75 ml) peanut oil
1 large onion, chopped
2 bay leaves
2 teaspoons dried oregano

Ask your butcher to saw the meat rather than chop it, or you will have unpleasant bone splinters throughout the flesh.

Pre-heat the oven to 200°C/400°F/Gas 6.

Put the meat into a deep roasting pan and cover with cold water. Add the other ingredients. Cover the pan with aluminium foil. Cook for 30 minutes and then reduce the heat to 130°C/230°F/Gas ½ for 2 hours.

You can serve it now, but it is much, much better if you let the meat cool in the liquid, perhaps overnight. Then, when you are ready to serve your Kleftiko, pour off the stock into a bowl and put the pan into a hot oven for 15–20 minutes until the meat is lightly browned. Present it with wedges of lemon, roasted potatoes and a green salad with some black olives, some tomato wedges, and a little crumbled feta cheese. The lamb-flavoured stock may be simmered with barley in it to make a delicious soup. It's even better if you brown the barley in a little oil in a pan first.

*Kleftiko is one of the stand-bys of the Greek Cypriot restaurants which have so proliferated during the last few years. This version is not the one usually found. A pity, for it's so much better. The secrets were given me by the Cleopatra Taverna in Notting Hill Gate.

MAIN COURSES

Mongolian Lamb

Serves 6 people

1 leg of lamb
1 oz (30 g) green ginger root
2 tablespoons clear honey
3 tablespoons fresh lemon
   juice
4 tablespoons soya sauce

Carefully slice off all the fat from the leg of lamb. Cut deep scores in a criss-cross pattern on both sides of the leg. Slice the green ginger into thin strips and stuff these evenly into the cuts.

Mix the three liquids well. Place the lamb in a roasting pan, pour over the marinade, and leave for at least 4 hours. Spoon the liquid over the meat as often as you can.

Pre-heat the oven to 150°C/300°F/Gas 2.

Cover the roasting pan with foil and cook the lamb for 20 minutes per pound (450 g). Take the pan out of the oven, remove the foil and slide the ginger pieces out of the meat. Baste it well, cover again with foil, and cook for 20 minutes more. Let the meat rest for 15 minutes out of the oven before you carve it. Serve with some of the marinade, but omit the pieces of ginger.

*This is adapted from a recipe normally used for very young venison, which has no fat. Older venison is also improved by this treatment. Even though the honey is likely to carbonise, this is wonderful cooked outdoors on a barbecue. Whether you roast or barbecue, the temperature must be low or the meat will shrink and be dry.

When first broadcast, this recipe attracted the greatest number of requests ever – more than 500 in the first two days!

MAIN COURSES

Trout Alhambra

Serves 4 people

4 trout, about ½ lb (225 g) cleaned weight, each
1 large orange
4 oz (110 g) leeks
½ pint (300 ml) red wine
3 dessertspoons clear honey
½ teaspoon cinnamon
½ teaspoon allspice
2 fresh bay leaves or 1 dried
salt and pepper
2 oz (60 g) butter

Take three strips of peel about 3 × 1″ (7.5 × 2.5 cm) from the orange. Remove the pith and cut the strips into long matchsticks. Slice the leeks very thinly indeed, including lots of the green. Throw orange sticks and leeks into boiling water and blanch until leeks just begin to wilt. Drain, then scatter the mixture on the bottom of an enamel or earthenware dish which is wide enough to hold the trout side by side. Make three slashes in the side of each trout, and lay them on top of the leek and orange mixture in the dish.

In a small saucepan, put the wine, honey, cinnamon, allspice and bay plus the juice of the orange. Bring slowly to the boil and simmer for 5 minutes. Thoroughly cleanse by straining through a very fine sieve or some muslin; pour over the trout in the dish. Salt and pepper the trout, then tilt the dish back and forth to ensure even distribution of the marinade. Leave, covered, for 2 hours at least.

Pre-heat the oven to 180°C/350°F/Gas 4.

Dot the fish with the butter. Cover the dish and bake 20–30 minutes according to the size of the fish and the thickness of the container.

*Based on the traditions of the Moors and the Levant, whence came much of English cooking, this unusual recipe may also be served cold, in which case omit the butter.

MAIN COURSES

Spiced Peaches

1 lb (450 g) firm peaches
8 dessertspoons white sugar
2 dessertspoons pickling spice
1 stick cinnamon
½ pint (300 ml) cider vinegar

Choose firm peaches, preferably only just ripe, as these will keep their shape better, and cut them into segments without skinning.

Put all the other ingredients together in a pan and bring to the boil very slowly. Simmer for 10 minutes. You can strain out the spices now, but I prefer to leave them in. Add the peach segments, bring gently back to the boil, and simmer for 8 minutes. Remove from the heat.

When thoroughly cool, first spoon the peaches into a clean screw-top jar, then add the liquid and spices. Store in a refrigerator until wanted. If you can bear the suspense, wait at least three days. Serve with tongue, ham, turkey or chicken, hot or cold. They make a fascinating addition to salads or mixtures of mayonnaise and cold poultry (see pages 34 and 35). Add a dessertspoon of vodka or brandy added to the pickle when it is cool would do no harm at all!

Tomato and Walnut Sauce

Serves 4–6 people generously

2 lb (900 g) ripe, red,
   flavourful tomatoes
4 tablespoons walnut oil (no
   substitutes)
2 cloves garlic, unpeeled
1 bay leaf
salt
1 teaspoon ground cinnamon
pinch cayenne pepper
6 oz (170 g) walnuts, ground
2–3 tablespoons red wine
   vinegar

Plunge the tomatoes into boiling water for 1 minute; drain, peel and de-seed them and chop roughly.

Heat the walnut oil gently in a thick-bottomed pan; add the tomatoes, garlic and bay. Cover and simmer with care for 45 minutes. Remove the bay and garlic and discard. Purée the tomato in a food processor or blender and force through a fine sieve.

Return the purée to the saucepan and flavour with a little salt, the cinnamon and the cayenne. Stir in the walnuts and complete the sauce by sharpening it with the red wine vinegar. Cook over low heat for 5 more minutes.

*The combination of tomatoes and walnuts is found in unexpectedly contrasting places – the Perigord and Armenia. This sauce combines the best of both of their cuisines, and it is one of my favourite creations. It's marvellous served hot or cold with chicken, turkey or lamb, and it really comes into its own used as a dip for cold meats on a picnic.

MAIN COURSES

Bolognese Sauce

Serves 4 people

1 large onion
½ stick celery
2 tablespoons olive oil, plus 1 teaspoon
1 lb (450 g) good quality beef, minced
2 × 14 oz (400 g) tins plum tomatoes
2 dessertspoons tomato purée
2 bay leaves
½ teaspoon salt

Finely chop the onion. String and chop the celery. Cook both in the 2 tablespoons oil in a saucepan for 10 minutes without browning, then add the meat. Turn continuously to break up and seal. Add the tinned tomatoes.

Fry the tomato purée in the teaspoon oil until a very bright red and starting to thicken further; it only takes a couple of minutes. Spoon some of the tomato juice from the saucepan into this. Stir well then pour it all back into the saucepan with the meat. Add the bay leaves and salt.

Leave to cook, covered, over a very low heat for at least 1 hour. Then tilt the lid so that excess moisture can evaporate, and continue to cook. When you can put a spoonful on a plate and no clear liquid separates out, it is ready.

Bolognese sauce should be very thick with the meat moist and succulent. If you want a thinner sauce, add some tomato purée, first fried as above and then thinned with a little wine or water. The frying maintains the bright redness.

*Use Bolognese sauce with any pasta. For a change, cook some tortellini – the meat-stuffed pasta that looks like belly-buttons. Add to this sauce and bake the lot in rich puff or short pastry. The result is really something. Or you could make Capelleti (page 42), stuffed with Bolognese sauce and served with more over the top and masses of grated Parmesan cheese.

Uncooked Cranberry Relish

4 oz (110 g) cranberries
1 small cooking apple
1 orange
½ lemon
½ lb (225 g) white or brown sugar

Mince or chop the cranberries rather finely, and do the same to the cored, peeled cooking apple.

Cut the unpeeled orange and lemon into pieces, and remove any pips. Mince the citrus finely too. Add to the cranberries, then mix in the sugar. Leave in the refrigerator at least 24 hours before using.

This relish lasts for weeks refrigerated; the addition of a capful of brandy improves both the flavour and the keeping properties.

Sweet Red Pepper Sauce, San Carlo

Serves 4 people

1 large onion
2 sweet red peppers
2 oz (60 g) butter
¼ pint (150 ml) white wine
fish or chicken bones
   (optional)
1 teaspoon tomato purée
½ pint (300 ml) double cream
salt and white pepper

Finely chop the onion. Quarter the red peppers and remove the seeds and stalk. Melt the butter and cook the onions and peppers together for 5 minutes. Add the wine and reduce gently to half the original quantity.

If you have some fish or chicken bones, simmer them gently in as little water as possible for 15 minutes; drain, then reduce that liquid to just a few tablespoons of strong stock. Add that to the onions and pepper.

Either way, now add the tomato purée, cook a few minutes and then liquidise the vegetables in a food processor or blender and strain well. Add the double cream and continue a gentle reduction over heat in an uncovered saucepan until you have a rich coating consistency. Complete the sauce with a little salt and white pepper; black pepper would spoil the appearance.

Serve with plainly steamed, baked or poached fish or chicken. (A chicken-stock based sauce will go with fish, but don't serve a fish-stock based sauce with anything other than fish.) This sauce is excellent with grilled lamb or veal chops too.

MAIN COURSES

*Nino Bergese was the Chef of Kings, King of Chefs, and created La Cucina Nuova, Italy's nouvelle cuisine. His exciting food is based on the disparate styles of Italian provincial food, creating the first truly national cuisine of that country. The San Carlo restaraunt in Highgate, London N.6, is the only place I know where you can find it; they gave me this recipe.

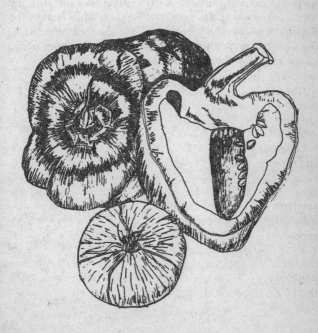

MAIN COURSES

Cranberry Sauce

1 lb (450 g) fresh or defrosted
   cranberries
¼ pint (150 ml) red or port
   wine
1 stick cinnamon
6–8 oz (170–225 g) white or
   brown sugar

Put the cranberries, wine and cinnamon into a saucepan and bring very slowly to the boil. Simmer just until the skins start to pop. Remove from heat. Add the sugar and stir gently until dissolved (if you add the sugar to the sauce while heating the berries, it will toughen the skins). Take out the cinnamon stick before serving hot or cold. Matchsticks of orange peel make a good addition to this sauce.

Cakes and Puddings

Tropical Banana Cake

6 oz (170 g) butter
9 oz (225 g) white sugar
3 eggs
3 medium to large bananas, mashed
3 tablespoons milk
1 teaspoon vanilla essence
3 rounded teaspoons baking powder
12 oz (340 g) plain flour

Filling
1 large banana
juice of ½ orange
up to ½ pint (300 ml) double cream, whipped

Chocolate Banana Icing
1 lb (450 g) icing sugar
1 large banana, mashed
melted butter
black rum (optional)
cocoa powder

Pre-heat oven to 180°C/350°F/Gas 4. Butter and flour a deep 8–9" (20–22.5 cm) cake tin.

Cream the butter and sugar in a large bowl, then beat in the eggs one at a time. Mash the bananas to a froth (use only those with a rich smell and mottled skin), then mix well with the butter/sugar mixture. Add the milk and the vanilla essence. Sift together the baking powder and the flour and

PUDDINGS AND CAKES

stir those into the mixture.

Pour into the tin and bake for 40–50 minutes or until a skewer inserted into the middle comes out clean. Cool 10 minutes in the tin, then turn out onto a rack to complete cooling.

Some people eat it like this, but for special occasions such as the Notting Hill Carnival, it should be filled and iced. First cut the cake in half. To make the filling, slice the bananas and soak in the orange juice. Drain and stir into the whipped cream (which may or may not be flavoured with black rum). Fill the cake and then make the tantalising icing.

The quantities of the last three icing ingredients will depend entirely on the size of the banana you have chosen, but if you expect *me* to get up early each Thursday to be in the studio, I think I can expect *you* to be creative here!

Mix the mashed banana into the icing sugar and gradually add melted butter, which should be warm rather than hot, to achieve a nice spreading consistency. Flavour the icing with some black rum if you like, then add cocoa powder to get rich colour and more flavour. Don't even consider using drinking chocolate powder. Spread over the top and sides of the cake, leaving the icing rough.

*This cake keeps for days and improves as it does so. If the chocolate-banana icing sounds too rich for you, the cake can be iced with a plain lemon, orange or chocolate icing.

If you've made banana cakes before, you might have noticed that a small amount of baking soda is often called for. This darkens the colour of the cake and emphasises the tiny brown flecks of the baked banana, but makes little difference to the flavour that I can discern. I think the pale yellow of my cake is infinitely more presentable.

Amazing Orange Cake

3 eggs
equivalent weight of the eggs
 in:
 butter
 sugar
 self-raising flour
fresh orange juice
1 teaspoon grated orange
 rind

Orange glaze
8 oz (225 g) sugar or icing
 sugar
¼ pint (150 ml) orange juice
1 teaspoon grated orange
 rind

This is a very old style of recipe (except for the self-raising flour, of course). The amount of orange juice needed depends on the size of eggs and the type of flour. But you can't go far wrong.

Pre-heat oven to 170°C/325°F/Gas 3, and line an 8–9″ (20–22.5 cm) cake tin with greased paper, which should come well above the rim.

Cream together the butter and sugar. Beat in the eggs one by one, then add the flour and mix well. Stir in fresh orange juice until you have a batter that is a little thicker than fresh double cream. Add the orange rind.

Pour into the cake tin and bake for 1 hour – it will take longer if you have made the mixture too wet.

While the cake cools in the tin for 10 minutes, prepare the glaze. Mix all three ingredients together until the sugar is dissolved. Turn the cake out on to a rack standing over a plate. Prick the surface of the cake with a fork or skewer, then

PUDDINGS AND CAKES

gently spoon the glaze over the cake, spooning back the excess until it is all absorbed.

Agonising though it will be, put the cake into an airtight tin and leave for three days before cutting. Serve each slice with some whipped cream.

*This cake used to be made for me by my Great-Aunt Rene, born on Norfolk Island, but who later lived in the country south of Auckland. When something good had happened, she would make an orange cake and send it up to Auckland by the rural bus service. It was the only time I wanted the buses *not* to run on time; the later they delivered the cake, the less time I had to stare hungrily at the tin before it was unsealed. The orange glaze can be used on almost any other cake; it may also have some orange juice replaced by a liqueur or brandy.

PUDDINGS AND CAKES

Chocolate Fudge Mud Pudding

Serves between 2 and 6 people!

2 oz (60 g) white sugar
4 oz (110 g) self-raising flour, sifted
½ teaspoon salt
2 oz (60 g) butter
1 oz (30 g) unsweetened dark chocolate
¼ pint (150 ml) milk
1 teaspoon vanilla essence
4 oz (110 g) dark brown sugar
4 tablespoons cocoa, sifted
generous ½ pint (300 ml) cold water

Pre-heat oven to 180°C/350°F/Gas 4.

Mix the sugar, flour and salt together. Melt the butter with the chocolate over low heat. Stir in the milk and vanilla. Let cool, then beat into the dry ingredients. Spoon this mixture into a deep baking dish.

Believe it or not, you now put the other ingredients on top of that!

Mix the sugar and cocoa together and spread evenly over the batter in the dish. Pour the cold water over the top.

Bake for 40 minutes, when the mud on the top will magically disappear. It reappears under the sponge-like pudding as a rich, sinful sauce. Let the pudding cool to warm before serving. With cream of course.

*This is a colonial echo of something from the English past. I've found similar recipes in New Zealand, on Pitcairn Island, in Boston, and in Katie Stapleton's book *Denver Delicious* where strong coffee is used instead of water – which gives you a Mocha Fudge Mud Pudding.

Peach Pie Royale

Serves 6 people

12 oz (340 g) short pastry
6–8 large, ripe, firm peaches
juice of ½ orange
2 dessertspoons sugar
2 teaspoons rosewater
2–3 oz (60–85 g) macaroons
  or amaretti
8–12 oz (225–340 g) puff
  pastry
food colouring (optional)

Pre-heat oven to 220°C/425°F/Gas 7. Line a 9" (22.5 cm) pie dish with the short pastry.

Plunge the peaches briefly into boiling water and peel them; cut into half or into large even segments if the clingstone variety. Toss in the orange juice to prevent discoloration, then drain.

Arrange the peaches on the pastry. Mix the sugar and rosewater together and sprinkle over the fruit. Lightly crush the macaroons or amaretti and pack around the edge of the pie and fill any other spaces between the peach pieces.

Cover with the puff pastry, using a pie funnel if you have one (slash the pastry several times if you have not). Decorate the pastry with the leftovers, if you like. In any case, you can achieve a right royal effect on this and all other baked pastry by painting on the surface with undiluted food colouring and letting it dry thoroughly before baking. Whether you simply paint stripes, write a name, or colour pastry leaves and roses, it creates a stunning effect. It is also the only authentic way to emulate the pastries of the medieval courts, which were coloured with sandalwood.

PUDDINGS AND CAKES

Pilgrim's Pudding with Butter Sauce

Serves 4–6 people

½ lb (225 g) raw cranberries,
   fresh or frozen
3 oz (85 g) butter
4 dessertspoons demerara
   sugar
2 teaspoons mixed spice
½ lb (225 g) self-raising flour
¼ pint (150 ml) molasses
⅛ pint (75 ml) milk
1 teaspoon vanilla or maple
   essence

Butter sauce
4 oz (110 g) butter
4 oz (110 g) sugar
¼ pint (150 ml) single or
   double cream
up to 2 teaspoons vanilla or
   maple essence (optional)

Butter a 3 pint (1.7 litre) pudding basin, and put 2 oz (60 g) of the cranberries, half the sugar and 1 teaspoon of the mixed spice on the base.

Roughly chop the remaining cranberries, leaving many of them cut no smaller than halves. Mix 4 oz (110 g) of them into the flour.

Warm your can of molasses by standing it in hot water, then measure out the required ¼ pint (150 ml). Add this to the milk, mix very well and add the vanilla or maple flavouring.

Mix the molasses liquid into the flour and turn into the pudding basin. Cover with remaining cranberries, sugar and mixed spice.

PUDDINGS AND CAKES

Seal the pudding basin in the usual way, with cloth or foil, remembering to fold a pleat in the top to allow for expansion. Steam on a trivet in a covered saucepan for 2 hours. Tip out of the basin to serve with the old-fashioned butter sauce.

Simply mix the sauce ingredients together in a small saucepan and simmer for 5 minutes. If you like, flavour with vanilla or maple essence.

*Many listeners wrote to say they had used this as their Christmas Pudding, for it is much lighter than the traditional recipe and can be made at the last minute. If you have to buy more than the ½ lb (225 g) cranberries needed, not to worry. They last for weeks in the refrigerator, and see also page 31.

PUDDINGS AND CAKES

Passion Fruit Paradise Pancakes

Serves 6 people

12 very thin pancakes
   (crêpes)
8 passion fruit
2 tablespoons white sugar
2 oz (60 g) butter
4 oz (110 g) caster sugar
juice of 2 large oranges and 2
   small lemons

Spoon the pulp from the passion fruit and mix with the 2 tablespoons sugar. Divide into two equal portions.

Squeeze and strain the juice of the oranges and lemons.

Use up one half of the passion fruit pulp by placing a teaspoonful in the middle of each pancake. Fold each in half and then in half again to make fan shapes.

Melt the butter in a wide pan; add the 4 oz (110 g) sugar and cook gently until it starts to caramelise. Beware of burning. Remove from the heat. Add the lemon and orange juices and the remaining passion fruit pulp. Cook until the sugar has dissolved again.

Lay the filled pancakes in the syrup, ensuring each is well covered. Simmer gently for 2 minutes, then serve 2 per person, with whipped cream.

*When I first made this, it was such a success I had to make another batch on the spot. It's piggy, but now I always double the recipe or invite only two other people!

South Pacific Ice Cream

Serves 4–6 people, accompanying fruit

3 small, very ripe bananas
1 teaspoon lemon juice, rum or orange liqueur (or more)
1 small tin sweetened condensed milk
¼ pint (150 ml) double cream
5 drops vanilla essence

Mash the bananas into a froth with lemon juice, rum or orange liqueur. Separately, beat the condensed milk until light, foamy and pale. Mix in the banana froth and then add the remaining ingredients. Beat with an electric beater for at least 2 minutes, longer if you can stand the noise. (A hand beater will take about 10 minutes.) The mixture should be the lightest, fluffiest possible.

Freeze in an ice cream tray or in a plastic container. There's no need to beat again, but if you do so when the outside of the ice cream is frozen but the centre is still mushy, you will have a lighter-textured ice cream.

Let soften slightly before serving with fresh fruit or a salad of tropical fruits.

*A word about bananas. Most people eat them far too green, which is both dangerous because of the acid content, and unpleasant because of the sting on the palate. In countries where they grow, bananas are only eaten when the skin is golden and mottled and the fruit perfumes any room they are in. The texture of the flesh is velvety and a glorious sweetness has developed. If I ever buy bananas in this country, I leave

PUDDINGS AND CAKES

them in a warm place for at least a week before I eat them. But if you ask your fruiterer for 'salad' or loose bananas, they are often much riper and can be eaten sooner. Unless you have perfectly ripe bananas – and it doesn't matter if they are a little bruised – don't make this ice cream. Unless you replace the bananas with a ripe mango. . . .

Jasmine Tea Ice Cream

Serves 4–6 people, meagrely

½ pint (300 ml) milk, plus a
　little more
1 oz (30 g) jasmine tea leaves
5 oz (140 g) sugar
1 level dessertspoon
　cornflour or arrowroot
2 egg yolks
pinch salt
½ pint (300 ml) whipping or
　double cream

Cornflour in ice cream? Yes. A cheat's recipe for those who don't trust themselves to make an egg custard without curdling it. If you are clever enough, omit the cornflour.

In any case, boil the milk and pour over the tea leaves. Let

PUDDINGS AND CAKES

brew for 9 minutes at the most, stirring occasionally. Strain well and make back up to ½ pint (300 ml) by adding a little more cold milk.

Mix the sugar, cornflour, egg yolks and salt together in a small saucepan then add the richly-coloured milk tea. Stir constantly until it boils and then reduce the heat and simmer for 5 minutes, or until all traces of flour flavour have vanished. (If you're not using cornflour or arrowroot, cook the mixture over a double boiler until it is a good custard consistency.)

Strain into a bowl, and cover the surface of the hot mixture with cling film. Cool.

Lightly whip the cream, blend it together with the cooled custard, and put into a suitable container. Freeze. The flour content prevents the ice cream from going icy; nonetheless, if you want to beat it lightly when it is half frozen, this will improve the texture.

Remove the ice cream from the freezer at least 30 minutes before serving. If you fancy a double delight of oriental flavouring, serve with a Lychee Sorbet (page 68).

PUDDINGS AND CAKES

Lady Tanlaw's Lychee Sorbet

Serves 4 people

1¼ lb (570 g) tin lychees in
   syrup
1–2 teaspoons rosewater
1 egg white

Open the tin of lychees and drain, reserving the syrup. Put the syrup into a saucepan and reduce gently by half; it will look slightly brown and taste as though caramelised.

Liquidise the lychees and put the purée through a strainer. Add the reduced syrup and stir in the rosewater. Remember that the sorbet will taste considerably less sweet when frozen, so don't be scared of injecting a moderately strong rose flavour now – later will be too late.

Put the purée to freeze and stir it from time to time. When almost frozen, quickly break it up and reduce to a purée again. If you have a food processor, so much the better. Then, fold in the stiffly beaten egg white and return immediately to the freezer.

A truly sublime way to end a rich meal when eaten by itself. Heavenly when served with a few slices of well-chilled caramel oranges, or with the Jasmine Tea Ice Cream.

*I cook for the Tanlaws' distinguished guests in London and Scotland, and I am allowed great freedom to invent and create. This was Lady Tanlaw's idea for a dinner in honour of His Excellency the Chinese Ambassador. Even before I started to work on the recipe, I knew it would both succeed and be a sensation. It did, and it is!

Japonais

Serves 12 people

Praline
6 oz (170 g) caster sugar
6 oz (170 g) hazelnuts or unblanched almonds

Meringue
12 oz (340 g) white sugar
6 egg whites

Crème au beurre
½ pint (300 ml) milk
4 oz (110 g) white sugar
6 egg yolks
14 oz (400 g) unsalted butter, softened
1 tablespoon coffee powder, dissolved in 1 tablespoon water

There are three things you must make to construct this masterpiece of French pâtisserie: praline, meringue and crème au beurre.

Praline. Put the caster sugar and nuts together in a thick-bottomed saucepan and set over a low heat. Do not stir. Heat gently. When the sugar begins to colour, stir with a wooden spoon until the nuts are toasted and the sugar a rich, golden brown. Pour immediately onto a cold, oiled metal baking sheet or onto a slab of marble.

When it is cold, break roughly or grind into a coarse powder, which is the more usual way of using praline (a food processor makes this a simple task). Keep praline in an airtight container for use in or on ice cream, cakes, hot or cold soufflés – or Japonais.

Meringue. First pre-heat the oven to 110°C/225°F/Gas ¼, then beat the sugar and egg whites together until standing in firm peaks. Divide the meringue evenly onto 3 × 9" (22.5 cm) circles of cooking foil or non-stick baking paper. Cook 8 hours – overnight is perhaps the easiest way. Invert, remove the foil or paper and let cool.

Crème au beurre. First, bring the milk and sugar almost to the boil and pour onto the 6 well-beaten egg yolks, stirring all the time. Cook the mixture in a double boiler until nice and thick – but before it curdles.

Take off the heat, cool to lukewarm.

Cream the unsalted softened butter with an electric beater, then slowly add that to the custard mixture. It will curdle if you are impatient and put too much in at a time. If it *does* curdle, beat in a couple of spoonfuls of *tepid* melted butter, which should bring it together again. When the butter is amalgamated, flavour the crème with lots of praline – at least half the above recipe – plus the strong coffee.

Japonais. Now for the final assembly! Divide the crème into four. Cement the 3 meringue layers together with 2 portions of the crème. Spread the third portion of crème evenly over the top. With a sharp knife trim the cake as evenly as you can. Mix the trimmings into the fourth portion of crème and use this to cover the sides of the Japonais. Make it as smooth as humanly possible; it will help if you heat the knife slightly in warm water.

Sprinkle more praline over the top and press some into the sides. Do not refrigerate, but keep it cool. Best made only a few hours before you wish to serve it.

---

*This recipe was taught me by an Eton schoolboy; he had extracted the recipe from an aunt, at the British Embassy in Paris, who took over a year to wheedle it from her local pâtisserie. It *is* difficult to make, and the crème *does* curdle easily. But if a 14-year-old, part-time cook can make it superbly, it must be possible for others to follow suit. So far, I haven't dared even show him my attempts. But here's a consoling thought. Few will ever have even seen one. However yours looks, it will taste as though you have slaved for days – as indeed you may have!

Buckingham Palace Strawberries

Serves 4 people

1 lb (450 g) strawberries
3 dessertspoons sugar
12 oz (340 g) raspberries (can be frozen)
juice of ½ orange
2–3 teaspoons rosewater
1 packet (about 4 oz or 110 g) sponge fingers
whipped cream
crystallised rose petals (optional)
Kirsch or Framboise eau-de-vie (optional)

If you really have to wash strawberries, do it before you hull them or you lose much of the flavour. Cut the hulled strawberries in half and sprinkle lightly with 2 dessertspoons of the sugar.

Make a purée of the raspberries and strain out the pips. Mix in the orange juice and remaining sugar. Don't make the raspberry purée too sweet, as it should contrast with the strawberries. Stir in the rosewater, remembering that it also has to be strong enough to flavour the strawberries.

Line the base of a smallish glass bowl with two layers of sponge fingers, sugary side down. Cover with strawberries. Pour over the purée, reserving a few tablespoons. Cover with more sponge fingers; press down slightly and spread the remaining raspberries evenly over the top.

Chill for at least 4 hours, then decorate the edges with whipped cream – I'd use ½ pint (300 ml); ¼ pint (150 ml) would do nicely. Scatter some crystallised rose petals on top.

*Some people who have borrowed this recipe found they preferred to add a little alcohol to the raspberries. Do, but don't use a sweet liqueur.

I planned this recipe during a private tour of the Palace's State Apartments in Jubilee Year. Only later did I learn that strawberries with a raspberry purée is a classic combination; the addition of rosewater is an inspiration thoroughly in keeping with those magnificent surroundings.

Other Strawberry Ideas

I agree strawberries with sugar and cream are wonderful, Wimbledon or not. But sometimes it is nice to serve them differently. Just so you can go back to sugar and cream again. Here are some of the ways of serving strawberries I have invented or discovered on my travels.

ORANGE STRAWBERRIES: macerate the strawberries in fresh orange juice for 30 minutes. Serve with cream.

ORANGE-FLOWER STRAWBERRIES: serve strawberries with a little sugar and cream into which you have mixed a few drops of orange-flower water, the distillation of the perfume of orange blossom.

MOCK CHAMPAGNE STRAWBERRIES: macerate sliced strawberries in dry ginger ale for 1 hour. Serve in long glasses with a long fork or spoon and top up with more ginger ale.

CHAMPAGNE STRAWBERRIES: macerate halved strawberries in an orange-flavoured liqueur. Place them in a long glass and top up with chilled champagne.

EXTRAORDINARY STRAWBERRIES: it's old-fashioned, but surprisingly good – grind some black pepper over strawberries. Otherwise sprinkle halved strawberries with sugar, add crushed mint leaves, and refrigerate for 2 hours. A salad of thinly sliced strawberries and cucumbers, beautifully arranged and dressed with the smallest amount of oil and lemon juice is always a surprise.

PUDDINGS AND CAKES

Caramelised Oranges

Serves 6 or more people

12 seedless oranges
1 lb (450 g) sugar
¼ pint (150 ml) water
½ pint (300 ml) orange squash,
   undiluted
brandy (optional)

Mix the sugar and water in a heavy-bottomed pan. Heat with care until it caramelises. When a rich brown, remove from the heat and add the squash. Keep your head out of the way for it will fizzle furiously. Return to the heat to allow the sugar to melt once more, then simmer 5 minutes. Check that any bitterness from the orange squash has disappeared; if not, cook a few minutes more. Let the syrup cool. If you have any cheap brandy, add up to ¼ pint (150 ml).

Peel the oranges with a long sharp knife, removing every piece of pith. Put whole into the orange syrup then leave in a cool place for 5–6 hours, or in a refrigerator for twice that long. Turn the oranges from time to time. The syrup will gradually change flavour as the orange juice and orange syrup mix together.

Although not essential, it is nice to make matchsticks out of some of the orange peel, ensuring that no trace of white is left. Plunge these into boiling water for 1 minute to remove bitterness, then drain.

To serve the caramelised oranges, slice each one thinly and arrange on pretty plates. Pour over some syrup and scatter some of the peel matchsticks on top. Lychee Sorbet as an extra topping is perfectly wonderful (page 68).

You will have extra syrup. Peel some more oranges and let them soak. Or use the syrup as sauce with South Pacific Ice Cream (page 65), for instance.

*I know the use of orange squash with real oranges is extraordinary. I was taught this by an Italian who owned a still sorely-missed restaurant in Marylebone. Try as I might I have never found a better alternative. If you're nervous about what guests might think, don't tell them . . . and hide the bottle.

Chinese Custard Tarts

Makes 24 tarts

1 lb (450 g) rich short pastry
2 large eggs
3 extra yolks from large eggs
½ pint (300 ml) milk
¼ pint (150 ml) single cream
4 oz (110 g) caster sugar

Pre-heat oven to 150°C/300°F/Gas 2, and ensure all filling ingredients are at room temperature.

Mix the eggs and egg yolks together thoroughly, but do not beat at a high speed or for too long. Add the milk, cream and sugar. Stir until the sugar is dissolved and let rest for 15 minutes.

Divide the pastry into 24 even pieces. Press each one into a patty or cup cake tin about 2½" (6.25 cm) diameter. Ensure the pastry is evenly spread and that it reaches right to the top of each container. Put the containers onto baking trays.

Gently spoon the egg and milk mixture into each, filling just to below the top. Cook for 45 minutes. Allow to cool for

PUDDINGS AND CAKES

15 minutes then gently loosen from the containers. They are best served warm.

*The Chinese call these Don Tot. The man in San Francisco's Chinatown who gave me the recipe added that the custard will curdle if the ingredients are not at room temperature when mixed. Should the custard start to bubble or brown during cooking, reduce the heat immediately; they must not brown like our custard tarts.

Index

Amazing Orange Cake, 58
Artichoke:
  Globe, Salmon Soufflé in, 16
  Jerusalem
    in Coronet of Smoked Oysters, 22
    Soup with Italian Dressing, 10
Asparagus Pastries with Maltese Sauce, 14
Aubergine, Baked with Noodles, 41

Baked Aubergine Noodles, 41
Beef Fillet with Mango, 36
Beef Paprikas, 44
Bolognese Sauce, 50
  in Capelletti, 42
Buckingham Palace Strawberries, 71
Buffet Food:
  Asparagus Pastries with Maltese Sauce, 14
  Chicken with Tarragon Pears, 35
  Coronet of Smoked Oysters, 22
  Green Peppercorn Mackerel, 18
  Green Peppercorn Salmon, 18
  Green Peppercorn Tuna, 18
  Holiday Pie, 30
  Jubilee Poultry, 33
  Moselle Chicken, 31
  Peachy Chicken, 34
  Pickled Salmon with Green Ginger Mayonnaise, 20
  Pink Cloud Pâté, 17
  Spiced Peaches, 48
  Three-Way Spiced Mackerel, 40
  Tomato and Walnut Sauce, 49
  Trout Alhambra, 47
  Turkey with Tarragon Pears, 35
  Uncooked Cranberry Relish, 51

Cakes:
  Amazing Orange, 58
  Tropical Banana, 56
Capelletti with Salmon Filling, 42
Caramelised Oranges, 74
Chicken:
  Moselle Chicken, 31
  Herby Chicken, 32
  with Tarragon Pears, 35
  Jubilee Poultry, 33
  Peachy Chicken, 34
  Chicken Paprikas, *see* Beef Paprikas
  Chicken with Tarragon Pears, *see* Turkey with Tarragon Pears
Chinese Custard Tarts, 75
Chocolate Banana Icing, *on* Tropical Banana Cake
Chocolate Fudge Mud Pudding, 60
Cinnamon, Parsnip and, Soup, 8
  Parsnip and, Sauce, 8
Clams, Souffléd Baby, 13

INDEX

Coronet of Smoked Oysters, 22
Cranberry:
   Sauce, 54
   Uncooked Relish, 51
   in Pilgrim's Pudding with Butter Sauce, 62
Cream of Fennel Sauce, *see* Cream of Fennel Soup
Cream of Fennel Soup, 12

Egg dishes:
   Holiday Pie, 30
   Salmon Soufflé in Artichokes, 16
   Souffléd Baby Clams, 13

Fennel,
   Cream of, Sauce, 12
   Cream of, Soup, 12
Fish:
   Mackerel,
     Green Peppercorn, *see* Green Peppercorn Tuna
     Three-Way Spiced, 40
   Salmon,
     Capelletti with Salmon Filling, 42
     Green Peppercorn, *see* Green Peppercorn Tuna
     Pickled, with Green Ginger Mayonnaise, 20
     Soufflé in Artichokes, 16
   Trout Alhambra, 47
   Tuna, Green Peppercorn, 18

Green Ginger Mayonnaise, *with* Pickled Salmon, 20
Green Peppercorn Mackerel, *see* Green Peppercorn Tuna
Green Peppercorn Salmon, *see* Green Peppercorn Tuna
Green Peppercorn Tuna, 18
Gremolata, Leeks in, 26

Herby Chicken, 32
Holiday Pie, 30

Ice Creams:
   Jasmine Tea, 66
   South Pacific, 65
Italian Dressing, Jerusalem Artichoke Soup with, 10

Japonais, 69
Jasmine Tea Ice Cream, 66
Jerusalem Artichoke Soup with Italian Dressing, 10
Jubilee Poultry, 33

Kleftiko Cleopatra, 45

Lady Tanlaw's Lychee Sorbet, 68
Lamb:
   in Kleftiko Cleopatra, 45
   Mongolian, 46
Leeks Aux Noix, 26
Leeks with Gremolata, 26
Limes, *in* Green Peppercorn Tuna, 18
Lychee, Lady Tanlaw's, Sorbet, 68

Mackerel:
   Green Peppercorn, *see* Green Peppercorn Tuna
   Three-Way Spiced, 40
Mango, Beef Fillet with, 36
Mayonnaise:
   Green Ginger, 20
   in Jubilee Poultry, 33
   in Peachy Chicken, 34

INDEX

Meringue, *in* Japonais, 69
Millefeuille, Saffron Seafood, 28
Mocha Fudge Mud Pudding, *see* Chocolate Fudge Mud Pudding
Mongolian Lamb, 46
Moselle Chicken, 31
Mushroom Stuffing, *in* Stuffed Kidney Cushions, 24

Noodles, Baked Aubergine, 71

Orange Glaze, *on* Amazing Orange Cake, 58
Oranges, Caramelised, 74
Oysters, Coronet of Smoked, 22

Pancakes, Passion Fruit Paradise, 64
Parsnip and Cinnamon Sauce, *see* Parsnip and Cinnamon Soup
Parsnip and Cinnamon Soup, 8
Passion Fruit Paradise Pancakes, 64
Pasta, *see* Capelletti
Pâté, Pink Cloud, 17
Peach Pie Royale, 61
Peaches:
  in Peach Pie Royale, 61
  in Peachy Chicken, 34
  Spiced, 48
Peachy Chicken, 34
Pears:
  Tarragon, with Turkey, 35
  Tarragon, with Chicken, *see* Turkey with Tarragon Pears
Pheasant, Spirited, 38
Pickled Salmon with Green Ginger Mayonnaise, 20

Picnic Food:
  Coronet of Smoked Oysters, 22
  Holiday Pie, 30
  Jubilee Poultry, 33
  Moselle Chicken, 31
  Pink Cloud Pâté, 17
  Spiced Peaches, 48
  Tomato and Walnut Sauce, 49
  Uncooked Cranberry Relish, 51
Pie:
  Holiday, 30
  Peach, Royale, 61
Pilgrim's Pudding with Butter Sauce, 62
Pink Cloud Pâté, 17
Pork Paprikas, *see* Beef Paprikas
Praline, *in* Japonais, 69
Prawns, Virginian, 23
Puff Pastry:
  in Asparagus Pastries with Maltese Sauce, 14
  in Holiday Pie, 30
  in Stuffed Kidney Cushions, 24

Rabbit with Gin and Juniper, 37

Saffron Seafood Millefeuille, 28
Salmon:
  Filling, Capelletti with, 42
  Green Peppercorn, *see* Green Peppercorn Tuna
  Pickled, *with* Green Ginger Mayonnaise, 20
Salmon Soufflé in Artichokes, 16
Sauces:
  Bolognese, 50
  Cranberry, 54

INDEX

Sauces *continued*

Cream of Fennel, *see* Cream of Fennel Soup
Maltese, 14
Parsnip and Cinnamon, *see* Parsnip and Cinnamon Soup
Sweet Red Pepper, San Carlo, 52
Tomato and Walnut, 49
Seafood Millefeuille, Saffron, 28
Shellfish:
Coronet of Smoked Oysters, 22
Pink Cloud Pâté, 17
Saffron Seafood Millefeuille, 28
Souffléd Baby Clams, 13
Virginian Prawns, 23
Smoked Oysters, Coronet of, 22
Souffléd Baby Clams, 13
Soufflés:
Baby Clams, 13
Salmon, *in* Artichokes, 16
Soups:
Cream of Fennel, 12
Jerusalem Artichoke, with Italian Dressing, 10
Parsnip and Cinnamon, 8
South Pacific Ice Cream, 65
Spiced Peaches, 48
Spirited Pheasant, 38

Strawberries:
Buckingham Palace, 71
Champagne, 73
Extraordinary, 73
Mock Champagne, 73
Orange, 73
Orange Flower, 73
Stuffed Kidney Cushions, 24
Stuffings:
Mushroom, in Stuffed Kidney Cushions, 24
Salmon Filling in Capelletti with, 42
Sweet Red Pepper Sauce San Carlo, 52

Three-Way Spiced Mackerel, 40
Tomato and Walnut Sauce, 49
with Herby Chicken, 32
Tropical Banana Cake, 56
Trout Alhambra, 47
Tuna, Green Peppercorn, 18
Turkey with Tarragon Pears, 35

Uncooked Cranberry Relish, 51

Virginian Prawns, 23

Walnut, Tomato and, Sauce, 49
Walnut Oil,
in Leeks Aux Noix, 26
in Tomato and Walnut Sauce, 49